I pray that this body of work inspires you to strive towards intentional togetherness, intentional communication, and intentional love.

xoxo
ShaVonne

Date _____

Dear

_____
_____
_____
_____
_____
_____
_____
_____
_____
_____
_____
_____
_____
_____
_____
_____
_____

Love,

Place a photo of your family here.

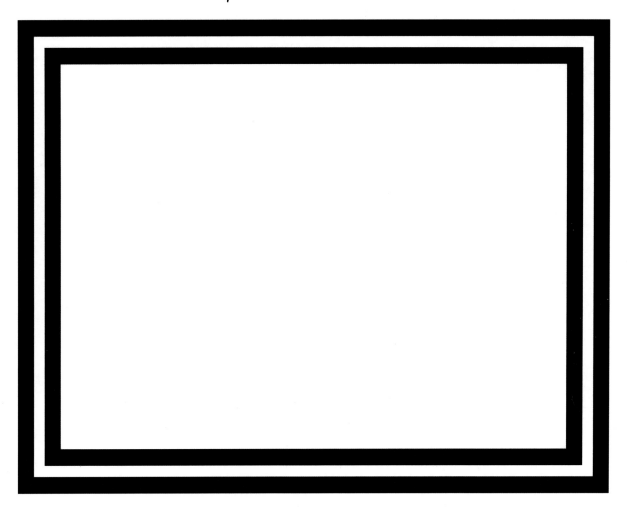

Family Name

LET'S EAT

Striving Towards Intentional Togetherness,
Intentional Communication, And Intentional Love

ShaVonne Cammack

FOREWORD BY CHEF YAKU

COOKBOOK

Book Cover By: Soleil Meade
Internal Layout: InSCRIBEd Inspiration, LLC.

Photography (c) 2020 by ShaVonne Cammack.
Additional photos used from Pexels.com and Unsplash.com:

Peaches: Photo by Katie Moum on Unsplash
Kids: @alyssasieb (IG)
Creative Commons — CC0 1.0 Universal
Steak: Photo by Adi Perets from Pexels
Veggies: Photo by Mark Stebnicki from Pexels
Popcorn: Free photo (Pexels)
Shopping Bags: @CreateHERStock
Creative Commons — CC0 1.0 Universal
Oats: Photo by Gaby Yerden on Unsplash
Rose: Kids: @alyssasieb (IG)
Creative Commons — CC0 1.0 Universal
Pancakes: Photo by Charles Deluvio on Unsplash
Pineapple Photo by Any Lane from Pexels
Flower Wall: Photo by Dids from Pexels

To my family:

My husband, my daughter, and my son.

Foreword: The Art of Breaking Bread

Often our greatest memories involve, or are somehow partnered with food. Some of my best memories growing up are holidays at my grandmother's house. Family sitting around the kitchen table cracking jokes and laughing, kids running around making noise and the smell of delicious food. I can vividly remember my grandmother in her own world, smiling from ear to ear as she watched us devour the food she spent all night and morning preparing. What was it that put such a smile on her face?

At that age, I didn't get it, I just knew I wanted to share that feeling. It wasn't until I had my own family that I realized what that feeling was. It was/is the art of breaking bread.

Food connects families, builds traditions and continues legacies, but it also connects friends. ShaVonne followed me on IG a few years ago and I followed her back. I began to notice very early that she not only cooked a lot, but it was obvious that she had a passion for cooking. Her homemade family meals were amazing and the stories that she shares with each post always made me reflect on some of my childhood memories.

The pressure that comes along with cooking produces a priceless reward, the camaraderie of family. This body of work not only gives you recipes to fill your belly, but the opportunity to build with your household and feel your soul. The simple act of cooking together has countless positive attributes that can make a lasting change with your family.

The stress of cooking can be calmed by the love of family, and togetherness. Get in the kitchen together, have fun, crack jokes, and remember, there's always pizza! I hope you and your family enjoy this journey through the art of breaking bread.

Chef Yaku
Food Network Star Season 12, Finalist
Cutthroat Kitchen Champion
NBC Food Fighters
D.O.P.E Chef Society
Kudachef@gmail.com

It Is What It Is

I am not a chef, nor am I a caterer, party planner, or restaurant owner. I am a wife and mother who strongly believes the act of breaking bread is one of the most valuable acts a family can do together. Breaking bread together aids in intentional togetherness which produces intentional communication and intentional love.

While navigating life as a wife and a mother I'm thrown curveballs consistently. Many women are faced with a preconceived notion that we are all supposed to know how to cook. I get it, the world wants us to accept gender roles and social norms, but I have always understood that being able to cook (at any level) is a necessary life skill. Some people, (notice that I did not specify gender), are naturally able to navigate the world of cooking, while others need guidance. If it is a homemade feast made from scratch or a frozen pizza, the intentional effort that goes into any meal should be celebrated. Like any skill, the more you practice it, the better you become.

I am confident that intentional actions feed our bellies and our souls.

Several times a day my family discusses what we plan to eat. We make a list of ingredients that are needed from the store, or if we want to order takeout, we decide where to order from. I am confident that this intentional communication feeds our bellies and our souls.

For years people have encouraged me to write a traditional cookbook, open a restaurant, start a catering business, or become a personal chef. I have always resisted those suggestions because God was clear that my purpose did not align with those things. He did however, tell me to create this body of work as a meal guide and recipe journal to encourage you to prepare home cooked meals with your family.

How many times have you followed a recipe, but changed a few things and it turned out perfectly? How many times have you remembered exactly what you did? The moral of this story is WRITE IT DOWN! I encourage you to put your unique spin on these recipes. Make sure you write down the following things to capture the historical and familial significance of your recipe:

1. The date and occasion
2. Special steps completed
3. Special ingredients added or removed

I want to emphasize that cooking is not about making the meal look exactly like a picture; it is more about the act of service to those that you are preparing the meal for, and or, with. As long as you and your family are fed and satisfied is all that matters. As you read, and write down your recipes and traditions, remember that perfection does not exist. This body of work is showing you alternate ways to prepare meals that can seem intimidating. Think about how to simplify tranditional recipes that are labor intensive. Utilize these recipes as templates, available to help you plan meals.

Oftentimes, we want to cook, but just don't know what to cook. Do the best with what you have. There are ways to substitute items that a recipe calls for with something you have in your panty. Over the years I have made some disgusting meals, and I was fully aware that the meals were not my best, however, my family would gather at the dinner table and devour my not so stellar meal as if it was prepared by an expert chef. Full disclosure; they did not have second helpings, but no one went to bed hungry. Those are funny memories that we look back at and laugh.

I pray that this journal helps you strive towards intentional togetherness, intentional communication, and intentional love.

XOXO

ShaVonne

Create The Ambiance

Have you ever had an amazing meal in the most unorthodox place? Have you ever had such a wonderful time at a dinner or lunch that the most mundane meal was strangely more delicious than it has ever tasted before? This type of psychological connection is intricately associated with the setting and ambiance of the space.

Did you know that a simple tablecloth and a bouquet of grocery store flowers or lighting a candle can also add to the ambiance. can transform a simple Sunday family dinner into a special occasion. Every grocery store that has a floral department, has discounted floral arrangements that they have to sell prior to their next shipment being delivered. The colors and simple design of the cloth coupled with the smell of the fresh flowers will create a lasting memory for everyone at the table.

When we host a guest in our home, it is customary for us to place a tray on the guest bedroom bed with the following items:

1. A small vase of flowers (does not have to be fancy, just something that speaks to your guest's personality. Some people arrive to a vase of roses, while others may arrive to find a vase of lilies)
2. A small bag or chips or popcorn. (It does not matter if your guests are traveling from across the country or next door, everyone like a nice crunchy snack.) Depending upon allergies, gourmet mixed nuts is always a good alternative to chips or popcorn. A small bag of candy such as chocolate or gummy bears.
3. A bottle of water.
4. An alcoholic drink, cup of coffee, or a cup of hot tea.

This exceedingly small detail shows your guests that you are intentional about their visit and they are welcomed into your home. Be sure to have fresh towels, spare toiletries, and extra pillows available if needed. At this point in thier visit you have not even served a meal and you have already established the ambiance with your guests.

Intentional communication opportunity:

Reach out to your guest prior to their arrival

To find out their like and dislikes.

Also find out their favorite snacks.

XOXO

My go-to charcuterie board is wooden and uniquely-shaped.

#letseatintentionally

Let's Eat

Charcuterie/Grazing Boards

Charcuterie boards have become popular for small gatherings and couch picnics. The key is to have a theme for your board and to pair items that have complimentary flavors. You can choose themes based upon holidays, sports teams, a date night or shareable appetizers for a meeting. Most deli sections in grocery stores have an area dedicated to everything you need to make a delicious charcuterie board. When you think you have too much, you don't.

Fine Cheeses
_____
_____
_____
_____
_____

Fine Chocolates
_____
_____
_____
_____
_____

Deli Meats
_____
_____
_____
_____

Gourmet Crackers
_____
_____
_____
_____

Pickled Snacks
_____
_____

Extras
_____
_____

Family Recipes and Notes

_____
_____
_____
_____
_____
_____
_____
_____
_____
_____
_____
_____
_____
_____
_____
_____
_____
_____
_____

Family Recipes and Notes

_____
_____
_____
_____
_____
_____
_____
_____
_____
_____
_____
_____
_____
_____
_____
_____
_____
_____

Be a smart shopper.
Make a list every time.

XOXO

Grocery Shopping 101

It is ironic how we have everything we need to be our best selves at our immediate disposal, but we must stop and take a full inventory of what we have. This notion also holds true for food. Doing the best with what you have can ensure that you are not being wasteful as well as teaching you creative ways to make meals unique. Prior to going grocery shopping, pick a day and thoroughly go through your pantry and refrigerator and take a full inventory of what you have. From this inventory create a list of possible meals. From there any gaps that you have will become your grocery list.

A little can go a long way if you plan, however do your best with what you already have in your pantry. If a recipe calls for elbow noodles and all you have is spaghetti, just substitute it, I promise you its not the end of the world.

Shop local/shop with small businesses as much as you can. You will find some of the best spices and organic produce at authentic markets and small family-owned grocery stores in town.

Order your groceries on-line and pick them up. You can't impulse shop because you can only order what's on your list. Some large grocery stores offer this service for FREE and you can use coupons. Look for print and digital coupons.

Notes
_____
_____
_____
_____
_____

Grocery List

Protein
_____
_____
_____
_____
_____
_____

Dairy
_____
_____
_____
_____
_____

Beverages
_____
_____

Extras
_____

Vegetables
_____
_____
_____
_____
_____
_____

Snacks
_____
_____
_____
_____
_____

Fruit
_____
_____

Special Requests
_____

Kitchen Staples and Must-Haves

There are a few things that you need to always have in your kitchen and in your pantry. Thrift stores and garage/estate sales are the perfect places to grab kitchen gadgets at affordable prices.

- Measuring cups/measuring spoons - For liquids and solids. You can not eye-ball everything and that is OK.
- Fresh Herbs - Only purchase fresh herbs the day that you are going to use them.
- Parchment paper or a reusable baking mat - For easy clean up and baked stuff will not stick to it.
- Corn starch - STOP using flour as a thickener.
- Broth - STOP using water, use broth to add flavor.
- Cast Iron pot/skillet - Preferably a skillet that is pre-seasoned.
- Wooden Spoon - Perfect for every meal.
- Deep Freezer - This is a great family investment.
- Blender - This multipurpose tool can be used to blend things, but it can also be a wonderful soup maker.
- Metal Spatula - A grilled cheese must have.
- Strainer - This multipurpose tool can be used to strain pasta and to wash produce.
- Mixer - Hand or stand, both work just fine.
- Freezer bags/vacuum sealer - Don't be wasteful, freeze for later.
- Food storage containers - Fall in love with leftovers.
- Sifter - Essential when baking and when working with powdered sugar.

Kitchen Staples and Must-haves for my Family

_____
_____
_____
_____
_____
_____
_____
_____
_____
_____
_____
_____
_____
_____
_____
_____
_____
_____
_____

Kitchen Staples and Must-haves for my Family

_____
_____
_____
_____
_____
_____
_____
_____
_____
_____
_____
_____
_____
_____
_____
_____
_____

A tittle can go a long way if you carefully plan.

#letseatintentionally

This is your base.
Add more or less of anything in each
blend including additional
salt as needed.

XOXO

Seasoning Blends

Cajun Blend

2 tbsp. Paprika
2 tbsp. Garlic Powder
2 tbsp. Oregano
1 tbsp. Kosher Salt
1 tbsp. Onion Powder
2 tsp. Ground Black Pepper
2 tsp. Cayenne *Omit if you don't like spicy flavor*

Mexican Blend

2 tbsp. Ground Cumin
2 tbsp. Chili Powder
2 tbsp. Paprika
2 tbsp. Dried Oregano
1 tbsp. Garlic Powder
2 tbsp Cayenne
Add 1 tbsp then taste before adding the 2nd, to determine your spice level

Italian Blend

3 tbsp. Basil
2 tbsp. Oregano
2 tbsp. Parsley
1 tbsp. Garlic Powder
1 tbsp. Onion (minced, dried)
1 tsp. Thyme
1 tsp Sage
1 tsp Rosemary
¼ tsp Black Pepper
¼ tsp Red Chili Pepper Flakes *Omit if you don't like spicy flavor*

Seasoning and Baking Needs

Garlic salt/garlic powder
Onion powder
Pink Himalayan sea salt
Fresh cracked black pepper
Seasoned salt
Paprika
Minced garlic
Butter
Olive oil/vegetable oil
Vanilla extract
Lemon extract
Cinnamon
Sugar
All purpose flour
Salted and unsalted butter
Sesame oil (essential for fried rice).

Always wear gloves when working with fresh jalapenos. Trust Me.

XOXO

Notes

_____
_____
_____
_____
_____

Common Measurements

Dash = less than 1/8 teaspoon
3 tsp. = 1 tbsp.
1 cup = ½ pint
2 cups = 1 pint
2 pints (4 cups) = 1 quart
4 quarts = 1 gallon (liquid)
16 oz. = 1 pound
4 tbsp. = ¼ cup
5 tbsp. + 1 tsp. = 1/3 cup
8 tbsp. = ½ cup
10 tbsp. + 2 tsp. = 2/3 cup
12 tbsp. = 3/4 cup
14 tbsp. = 7/8 cup
16 tbsp. = 1 cup

Metric Measurements

1 teaspoon = 5 ml
1 tablespoon = 15 ml
1/4 cup = 60 ml
1/3 cup = 80 ml
½ cup = 120 ml
2/3 cup = 160 ml
3/4 cup = 180 ml
1 cup = 240 ml
1 quart = (4 cups) 1 liter
1 gallon = 4 quarts
½ ounce = 15 g
1 ounce = 30 g
3 ounces = 85 g
4 ounces = 115 g
8 ounces = 225 g
12 ounces = 340 g
16 ounces = 455g (1 lb.)
2 pounds = 1 kg

Must-have Seasonings for my Family

_____

_____

_____

_____

_____

_____

_____

_____

_____

_____

_____

_____

_____

_____

_____

_____

_____

_____

_____

_____
_____
_____
_____
_____
_____
_____
_____
_____
_____
_____
_____
_____
_____
_____
_____
_____

Notes About Seasonings

Never cook a cold steak,
always cook it at room temperature.

#letseatintentionally

Well-seasoned and flavorful does not mean salty.
Pay attention to the sodium in all of your ingredients.
Taste as you cook.

XOXO

Family Kitchen Tips and Notes

Family Kitchen Tips and Notes

_____

_____

_____

_____

_____

_____

_____

_____

_____

_____

_____

_____

_____

_____

_____

_____

_____

_____

_____

Family Kitchen Tips and Notes

_____
_____
_____
_____
_____
_____
_____
_____
_____
_____
_____
_____
_____
_____
_____
_____
_____
_____

The Most Complex Meal of the Day

 While most people say that breakfast is the most important meal of the day, I say that it is the most complex meal of the day. We want our kids to eat a hearty meal before school, however, we do not have time to prepare an "All Star" breakfast on a regular Tuesday. The breakfast meal ideas in this section can easily be prepared in advance to aid in a smooth morning routine. Please encourage your children to make their own meal choices when they can, and allow them to prepare their meals themselves.

Breakfast on the go ideas for my family:

_____

_____

_____

_____

_____

_____

_____

_____

_____

_____

_____

BREAKFAST

Give yourself a break.
Breakfast pastries and milk are okay.
A cupcake is okay. No judgment.

#letseatintentionally

Be intentional in all that you do,
you never know how big of an impact the smallest
gesture can have on a person's entire life.

XOXO

Peaches

When I was a young child, my great aunt and I took a charter bus from Omaha, Nebraska to West Virginia, to visit my mother, who I had not seen in almost a year. My great aunt and I stayed at a beautiful, traditional Bed & Breakfast (B&B), I can vividly remember it like it was yesterday. The B&B had shiny brown hard wood floors that made me feel like I was walking on bars of chocolate. Each room was beautifully decorated with plush area rugs, rich burgundy curtains, and gorgeous handmade quilts covered the enormous Victorian style beds. Everything about the experience was foreign to me and I felt anxious. As a child I was able to associate my uneasy feelings with the unfamiliar surroundings, and the thoughts of the scary experience that awaited me the next day.

I can't recall what we ate for dinner that night, but I remember still feeling anxious when I woke up the next day. When I sat at that kitchen table for breakfast, the sweet, older lady who owned the Bed and Breakfast placed a small bowl of frosted shredded wheats in front of me and said, "Early this morning I went out to my orchard and picked two peaches just for you." She diced up one peach and added it to my cereal, then told me to take the other one with me. I later learned that I was so nervous about the upcoming experience that I had wet the bed the night before. The sweet lady did not want me to feel embarrassed about my accident, or nervous about seeing my mom, so having the peach that was specially picked just for me served as a welcome comfort. To this day it is my lifelong dream to own and operate a Bed and Breakfast, and I still enjoy peaches in my cereal.

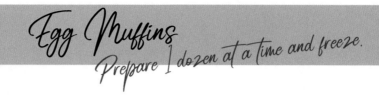

Egg Muffins

Prepare 1 dozen at a time and freeze.

5 eggs
2 tbsp milk
½ cup grated cheddar cheese
½ cup protein of your choice cut into small pieces (I use prepackaged turkey sausage crumbles)
½ cup green bell pepper
¼ cup white onion
½ tbsp olive oil
(Once frozen, microwave defrost for 1 minute, microwave heat for 1 min and enjoy)

1. Spray mini muffin pan generously with cooking spray
2. Preheat oven to 350° F
3. Heat oil in skillet.
4. Add protein, red or green pepper and white onion, cook until peppers and onion are slightly tender.
5. In separate bowl whisk together, eggs, milk, and grated cheese.
6. Stir protein mixture into egg mixture.
7. Pour into greased mini muffin pan.
8. Bake 350 for about 15-20 minutes or until golden brown.

Notes
_____

_____

Quiche

4 eggs
Your choice of add-ins: crumbled bacon, sausage, veggies, onions…
(Sautee veggies and protein prior to assembly)
9-inch-deep dish frozen pie crust
Shredded cheese
1 cup of milk
Your choice of seasonings. (My go-to is salt, pepper, paprika, parsley)

1. Pre-heat your oven to 400 degrees
2. Combine eggs and add ins. Pour egg mixture into pie dish.
3. Bake for 15 minutes.
4. Lower oven temperature to 350 and bake for 35-40 more minutes.

Notes
_____
_____
_____
_____
_____
_____
_____
_____
_____
_____
_____

Breakfast Burrito

Scrambled eggs
Protein of choice
Shredded cheese
Salsa
Sour Cream
Flour Tortillas

Put all ingredients into your flour tortillas and enjoy!

Notes

_____
_____
_____
_____
_____
_____
_____
_____
_____
_____
_____
_____
_____

Breakfast Sandwich Ideas

Sausage Hash Brown Casserole

1 lb breakfast sausage (pork or chicken)
½ small red bell pepper
1/3 white onion
½ small green bell pepper
1 lb frozen hash browns
½ cup sour cream
½ tsp. garlic salt
½ tsp. salt & pepper
4 eggs
¼ cup milk
1 cup cheese shredded (I used a mixture of cheese, typically whatever is on sale)

1. Preheat oven to 375 F.
2. In a large skillet cook sausage until browned. Place the sausage on paper towels to drain. Leave the fat in the skillet.
3. Dice up the onions, green bell pepper, and red bell pepper.
4. Add to skillet and sauté until just tender
5. Place the sautéed veggies on a plate and set aside.
6. In a large bowl add the THAWED, hash browns.
7. Stir in the sour cream until it coats the hash browns
8. Stir in the processed cheese.
9. Season with salt, pepper and garlic powder. (Taste the mixture to make sure the seasonings are just right. Be careful not to over-season, since you are also using sausage and cheese)
10. Spray a 9 inch deep dish pie plate with cooking oil and press the hash brown mixture into the pie plate getting it as flat and even as possible.
11. Cover the top with sausage, onions and peppers. Set aside.
12. In a small bowl beat eggs with milk.
13. Pour the egg mixture evenly over the top of the casserole. (Use a knife to poke holes in the casserole so that the eggs mixture goes down further)
14. Top with shredded cheese.
15. Cover with foil and bake for 45 minutes.
16. Remove the foil and bake for another 10-15 minutes or until the casserole is fully set.
17. Let cool for 10 minutes and enjoy!

 Notes
_____

Mini Pancakes

1¼ cups all-purpose flour
1 tsp. baking powder
1 tsp. baking soda
1/8 tsp. salt
¼ cup granulated sugar
1 egg room temperature
3 tbsp. unsalted butter melted
½ tsp. vanilla extract
1¼ cups buttermilk warm
*I like to add a pinch of cinnamon

1. In a medium-size bowl, whisk or sift flour, baking powder, baking soda, salt and sugar until well combined. Set aside.
2. In a large-size bowl, whisk together egg, butter, vanilla extract and buttermilk until combined.
3. Add dry ingredients into wet ingredients until batter is smooth with a few lumps.
4. Let batter rest for 10 minutes.
5. Heat and lightly butter a nonstick griddle/skillet.
6. When the griddle/skittle is hot, using a mini cookie scoop, scoop out a tablespoon-size amount of batter.
7. Place batter on hot skillet and cook until bubbles begin to break on the surface and the underside is golden.
8. Flip the pancakes and cook until other side is golden.
9. Place pancakes on a cooling rack to cool. Do not stack while they are hot.
10. Brush hot pancakes with butter and serve with warm maple syrup. (Do not brush with butter if preparing in advance to freeze)

Prepare pancakes in advance
and freeze them in a double freezer bag.
#letseatintentionally

Sausage Gravy

1 lb ground turkey or pork sausage
1 tbsp. olive oil
1 ½ tsp. seasoning salt
½ tsp. paprika
1 tsp. black pepper
2 tsp. brown sugar
½ tsp minced garlic
Pinch of celery salt (optional)
½ tsp. dried oregano
1 tsp. sage
Generous pinch of red pepper flakes (optional)
¼ cup flour
4 cups warm milk (more or less depending on how thick or thin you prefer it)
*You can substitute seasonings and use your favorite breakfast sausage**

1. In a large bowl add ground sausage and olive oil.
2. Mix together all of the seasonings in a small bowl.
3. Pour seasonings over ground meat and mix until well distributed.
4. Fry a small piece of the sausage mixture to make sure it is flavorful and adjust seasonings if needed.
5. In a large deep skillet, add in sausage and cook over medium heat until browned. Break the sausage up as it cooks.
6. Drain the excess fat from the pan if needed, but leave about a tablespoon of fat in the pan.
7. Sprinkle flour over cooked sausage a little at a time until all of the flour has been absorbed.
8. Continue cooking the sausage for a couple more minutes to cook out the flour taste.
9. Gradually add the warm milk, stirring constantly.
10. Allow gravy to come to a light simmer while stirring and reduce heat.
11. Continue stirring until desired consistency is reached.
12. (If you need to thin out the gravy add more milk. If you need to thicken the gravy, simply allow it to cook a bit longer. Remember the gravy will thicken more as it cools.)
13. Remove from heat.
14. Season to your liking with salt (if needed), black pepper, to bring out the flavor of the gravy.
15. When tasting the gravy for seasoning, be sure to sausage in your taste test to prevent over salting the gravy.
16. Serve piping hot over homemade biscuits. (See biscuit recipe page 44)

French Toast

6 slices of Brioche bread (toast lightly)
(This ensures that your French toast will not be soggy)
3/4 cup warm milk (I like to use egg nog during the holiday season)
2 tbsp. all-purpose flour
1 tbsp. vanilla extract
1 tsp. cinnamon
2 tbsp. brown sugar
2 tbsp. melted butter
2-3 eggs yolks

1. Mix together warm milk and flour until flour is dissolved.
2. In a small bowl stir together vanilla and cinnamon and add to milk-flour mixture.
3. Stir in brown sugar and melted butter.
4. Add in egg yolks and mix until well combined.
5. Pour batter into a 9 x 13 casserole dish.
6. Dip both sides of bread until moist but not dripping or completely saturated.
7. Place bread on a cookie sheet while griddle/skillet is heating.
8. Add butter to griddle/skillet and heat over medium heat.
9. When griddle/skillet is hot, place bread on griddle.
10. Cook until golden, flip and cook the other side until golden.
11. Serve hot, sprinkled with powdered sugar, butter and warm maple syrup.

Chocolate Gravy

1/3 cup unsweetened cocoa powder
3 tbsp. all-purpose flour
1 cup sugar
1 pinch salt
1 ½ cups milk
3 tbsp. butter
1 teaspoon vanilla extract

1. In a medium saucepan, whisk together the cocoa powder, flour, sugar, and salt.
2. Pour in the milk and whisk until all the lumps are gone.
3. Place the pan over medium heat and cook 5 to 7 minutes, stirring constantly, until the gravy just begins to boil and then thickens.
4. Once thick, remove from the heat stir in the butter and vanilla.
5. Stir until the butter has melted. Serve over hot biscuits (page 44)

Notes

Buttermilk Biscuits

These are a staple in my house.

2 cups self-rising flour
½ tsp. salt
2 tbsp. light brown sugar
1 cup buttermilk (cold)
¼ cup cold heavy whipping cream
6 tbsp. salted butter super cold
2 tbsp. butter-flavored
cold vegetable shortening

1. Preheat oven to 450 F.
2. Line a cookie sheet with parchment paper/baking sheet. Set aside.
3. In a large bowl add flour, salt and brown sugar. Whisk till combined.
4. Grate the cold butter into the flour mixture and add the shortening.
5. Use a fork, whisk or pastry cutter to cut the butter and shortening into the flour mixture until it resembles large crumbs.
6. Make a well in the center of the bowl.
7. Mix together the buttermilk and heavy cream.
8. Add to the center of well.
9. Slowly and very gently begin adding the flour mixture into the well.
10. Stir gently until the flour mixture is moistened (do not over stir)
11. Generously flour your work surface with flour.
12. Place dough onto floured surface.
13. Sprinkle the top of dough with flour and flour your hands as well.
14. Very gently, knead the dough by folding it in layers a few times while adding more flour, just enough so that the dough is not sticking to your hands or your work surface. (less flour, the better)
15. Gently pat the dough out into a small rectangle about 1 inch thick.
16. Flour your biscuit cutter and cut out circles.
17. Place biscuits on prepared cookie sheet with sides barely touching.
18. Make a small dent in the center of each biscuit with your finger (this helps tall biscuits rise without falling over)
19. Bake for 10-12 minutes or until golden. (Adjust cooking time according to your oven. DO NOT PUT THEM IN AND WALK AWAY) Brush with melted butter as soon as they come out of the oven. (DO NOT SKIP THIS STEP)
20. Serve hot.

Overnight Oats

My family enjoys when I warm it in the microwave for a minute.

½ cup old-fashioned oats (NOT quick oats)
½ cup milk (whichever type you prefer)
½ tsp pure maple syrup
¼ tsp pure vanilla extract

1. Combine oats, milk, maple syrup and vanilla in a mason jar or bowl.
2. Seal with a lid and shake to mix or stir if using a bowl. (If making a larger batch, stir the ingredients together in a bowl.)
3. Refrigerate overnight or at least 6 hours and up to 4 days.
4. Before serving, stir and add any preferred toppings such, dried fruit, honey, almonds, a banana, nuts, etc.
5. Add butter and a pinch of cinnamon.

Notes
_____
_____
_____
_____
_____
_____
_____
_____
_____
_____

Loaded Yogurt

Yogurt (Greek, almond, regular, fruit)
Toppings: fresh fruit, granola, agave, gummy bears/worms, brown sugar, cinnamon, chocolate chips

This is an extremely fun meal that allows everyone to load up their own individual cup of yogurt or hot cereal with fresh fruit, granola, honey, brown sugar, or gummy treats.

Notes

_____
_____
_____
_____
_____
_____
_____
_____
_____
_____
_____
_____

Breakfast Favorites

Breakfast Favorites

_____
_____
_____
_____
_____
_____
_____
_____
_____
_____
_____
_____
_____
_____
_____
_____
_____
_____

Breakfast Favorites

_____
_____
_____
_____
_____
_____
_____
_____
_____
_____
_____
_____
_____
_____
_____
_____
_____
_____

Breakfast Favorites

_____
_____
_____
_____
_____
_____
_____
_____
_____
_____
_____
_____
_____
_____
_____
_____
_____

Breakfast Favorites

_____
_____
_____
_____
_____
_____
_____
_____
_____
_____
_____
_____
_____
_____
_____
_____
_____
_____
_____

Watching Mothers

My parents were never married, so I did not grow up watching my mother in a wife capacity. I always say, "Create the life that you want to live!" As a little girl, I used to dream about the life that I currently live. My dreams were very clear. However, they did not include specifics like the size of my home, the make or model of the car I would drive, or what career I would have. My dreams always depicted me as a matriarch of a family. Most, if not all my dreams were in a kitchen preparing a meal or at a table having a meal with my family. Not having the daily visual within my home, but dreaming about being a wife and mother, I learned from TV wives, how to "wife." I learned from Clair Huxtable that it is perfectly "OK" to work outside of the home and for my husband to also prepare meals for the family. From Florida Evans I learned that as long as my family has a hot meal available for them, they do not care about fancy ingredients or expensive china. Lastly, I learned from Weezie Jefferson that being a perfect cook is not a requirement to be a good wife/mother.

Preparing meals with, and for my family is important to me because it serves as the nucleus of daily communication.

#letseatintentionally

Food is Good Anytime

Breakfast food for breakfast, late lunch, late dinner, or breakfast for dinner, whatever you decide to prepare, at whatever time you decide is fine.

APPETIZERS, MAIN DISHES & OTHER STUFF

Whatever you decide to prepare is fine at whatever time you decide to eat.

XOXO

Beef Tips and Gravy

1 tbsp. butter
3/4 cup onions diced
2-3 tsp. garlic minced
2 lbs beef tips (Stew meat)
olive oil for lightly coating beef
1 tsp. salt
1 tsp. black pepper
1 tsp. garlic powder
1 tsp. onion powder
1 tsp oregano
2½ cups beef broth divided
¼ tsp. red pepper flakes
½ tsp. rosemary
½ tsp. oregano
½ tsp. sage
½ tsp. thyme
1-2 tbsp. steak sauce or Worcestershire sauce
1 bay leaf
¼ cup cornstarch

1. Melt butter in a large cast iron or deep skillet.
2. Add onions and sauté until tender.
3. Add garlic and cook until fragrant and golden, do not burn.
4. Remove onion and garlic from skillet and set them aside.
5. Season beef generously with salt, black pepper, garlic powder, onion powder, and oregano.
6. Heat the skillet over high heat and add the beef in a single layer.
7. Sear the outside just until brown and slightly crisp
8. Remove beef from pan.
9. Pour ½ cup of beef broth into the hot pan to de-glaze the pan and loosen up all the stuck-on pieces.
10. Stir in remaining broth, reserved onions and garlic, red pepper flakes, rosemary, oregano, thyme, sage and steak or Worcestershire sauce.
11. Simmer for 10-15 minutes.
12. Add in the beef and bay leaf.
13. Cover and simmer for 60-90 minutes or until beef is cooked through and tender. (may need shorter or longer cooking time)
14. To thicken the gravy, remove 1 cup of broth from the pan and place in a bowl.
15. Add the cornstarch to the bowl and stir until smooth. DO NOT ADD THE CORNSTARCH DIRECTLY INTO THE PAN.
16. Pour the broth-cornstarch mixture back into the pan and stir.
17. Cover and simmer for 5-10 minutes until the broth has thickened.
18. Taste and add additional seasonings if desired.
19. Serve hot over steamed rice or garlic mashed potatoes.

Easy Party Dip

You can substitute fresh vegetables in place of tortillas.

(2) 8 oz bars cream cheese, room temperature
3/4 cup sour cream
½ cup mayonnaise
3/4 tsp. chili powder
3/4 tsp. garlic powder
3/4 tsp. onion powder
1 tsp. parsley
1 ½ cups Colby Jack cheese
1 ½ cups mild cheddar cheese
½ cup mozzarella cheese
1 lb bacon cooked and chopped into bits (turkey bacon is fine)
(1) 4 oz can diced jalapenos
8 tbsp. butter
Tortilla chips

1. Preheat oven to 350 F.
2. In a large bowl cream together cream cheese, sour cream, and mayo.
3. Add in chili powder, garlic powder, onion powder, and parsley.
4. Stir in 1 cup Colby Jack and 1 cup mild cheddar.
5. Reserve ¼ cup of the bacon and stir in the rest.
6. Stir in the Jalapeños.
7. Taste mixture and add in additional seasoning if desired.
8. Pour mixture into a casserole dish and spread into an even layer.
9. Mix remaining cheese and sprinkle on top. (½ cup Colby jack, ½ cup cheddar, ½ cup mozzarella)
10. Pour mixture into a casserole dish and spread into an even layer.
11. Mix remaining cheese and sprinkle on top. (½ cup Colby jack, ½ cup cheddar, ½ cup mozzarella)
12. Sprinkle on the reserved bacon and enough parsley to make it pretty.
13. Bake for 25-30 minutes until cheese has melted.
14. When dip is done remove from oven and let cool for a few minutes.
15. Lay a paper towel on the top and press gently to soak up the oil.
16. Serve the dip hot with the tortilla chips.

Notes
_____
_____
_____
_____
_____
_____
_____

Grandma's Wisdom

I often find myself thinking of food in ways that most people do not. While I love the taste of delicious food, my psychological connections to various meals, which triggers memories, drives my tastebuds. For example, I crave salmon croquettes when I think of my great grandmother Betty. She first introduced me to these delicious fish cakes when I was a child. I remember sitting at her tiny two seat kitchen table, next to the open window watching her carefully remove the pink salmon from the can and effortlessly taking out the bones. She was always careful not to add too much salt because she used crumbled saltine crackers to bind the salmon, eggs, and seasonings. Every now and then she would get so distracted by one of her daytime "stories" on TV that she would add too many crackers, making the salmon mixture too dry.

Fear not, the lesson she taught me was to add a splash of milk or broth if this happens. This trick also works for meat loaf. This connection to my great grandmother has transcended into my adulthood, as I am always looking to generate a memory through an experience with food.

Salmon Croquettes

2 can (14 oz.) pink salmon
1 medium onion finely chopped fine.
1 medium green bell pepper chopped fine.
2 large eggs, beaten
½ cup yellow cornmeal
1tsp. lemon juice
¼ cup mayo
½ cup Italian bread crumbs
1tbsp Cajun Blend (see seasoning section above)
2 tbsp butter or extra virgin olive oil

1. Drain juice from salmon.
2. Pour salmon into a medium bowl and using a fork break salmon apart into small pieces and remove bones.
3. In a separate bowl, mix all other ingredients thoroughly.
4. Add salmon to mixture, shape the mixture evenly into patties.
5. Place patties in freezer for 30 minutes to tighten.
6. Heat the butter or oil over medium heat in a medium skillet. Brown salmon croquette patties on both sides, 3-5 minutes on each side.
7. Serve salmon croquettes hot.

Notes
_____

Cultivating a Village

Armed with my premature cooking skills and common sense, I began my undergraduate college journey in the small city of Normal, AL. I quickly learned that having limited funds and a lack of family close by was going to immediately put those cooking skills and common sense to the test. Prior to becoming a wife and a mother, I learned how to do more with less as a broke college student.

Living off my tuition refund checks and food stamps, I was able to feed myself as well as several of my friends. We could not afford to have pizza delivered or visit restaurants often, but we could pull together homecooked meals that everyone was welcome to come by and enjoy. I later learned that some of those meals were the only daily meals my friends had at that time.

Providing breakfast before someone ran off to take their final exam, or pulling together a modified holiday meal because some of us could not always travel home to be with our families during those days, was normal for me and our village. These intentional meals set the tone for the rest of my adult life. Something special happens when you feed a person's belly and their soul.

I am always looking to generate a memory through an experience with food.

#letseatintentionally

Loaded Taco Soup

If you have leftover flour tortillas from Taco Tuesday, make grilled cheese quesadillas and Taco soup.

1 lb. ground beef/ground turkey
(1) 15.25 oz can Rotel tomatoes
(1) 15.25 oz can beans, drained canned *I prefer pinto or black beans*
(1) 15.25 oz can sweet corn
Mexican seasoning blend to taste (see seasoning blend section p. 16)
1 package of dry ranch dip/seasoning
1-2 cans of water

Topping Options: Green onion slices, Diced avocado, Sour cream, Shredded cheese, Jalapeño slices, tortilla strips

1. Brown ground beef/turkey in large dutch style pot.
2. Cook until ground meat is done and then drain off the fat.
3. Add in all remaining ingredients.
4. Cover and simmer for 30 minutes.
5. Taste and add additional seasonings if needed.
6. Spoon into bowls and top with desired toppings.

Notes
_____
_____
_____

Tuna Casserole

(1) 5 oz. can of light tuna, drained
(1) 10 oz can of Cream of Celery soup
8 oz. egg noodles
½ tsp. salt plus extra to taste
3 tbs salted butter
½ tsp. pepper
½ tsp. garlic powder
1 ½ cups shredded cheddar cheese, divided
3/4 cup frozen peas
2 tbsp. crushed plain (salted) potato chips

1. Preheat oven to 350° F.
2. Coat bottom and sides of baking dish with butter or spray with non-stick coating.
3. Cook the egg noodles according to package directions in heavily salted water. Drain and transfer to buttered baking dish. Set aside.
4. In a separate bowl, mix tuna, cream of celery soup, Stir in salt, pepper, garlic powder, frozen peas and ½ cheddar cheese.
5. Bake for 15 minutes, remove, top with remaining cheese and potato chips.
6. Bake for an additional 10 minutes and serve while hot.

*Any day is a good day
for a grilled cheese sandwich.*

XOXO

Snap a pic of a dish you have made and place the photo here.

Vegetable Stew

Frozen vegetables work just fine.

2 tablespoons olive oil
3/4 cup onions diced
1 cup celery diced
1 ½ cups carrots diced
3 tsp garlic minced
2 ½ cups yellow potatoes peeled and diced into small cubes
2 14.5 oz can diced tomatoes
1 cups green beans
6 ½ cups of broth (chicken, beef, vegetable)
½ can (46 oz.) tomato juice (use more if desired)
1 ½ teaspoons oregano
1 ½ teaspoons basil
1 teaspoon thyme
1 teaspoon parsley
1 bay leaf
1 ½ cups corn
1 ½ cups sweet peas
salt pepper, garlic powder, cayenne pepper and onion powder, to taste.

1. In a large pot, heat olive oil over medium heat.
2. Add in onion, celery, and carrots.
3. Cook until carrots are slightly tender to the bite.
4. Add in garlic and cook until fragrant.
5. Add in potatoes, tomatoes, and green beans.
6. Pour in broth and tomato juice.
7. Stir in oregano, basil, thyme, parsley, and bay leaf.
8. Bring to a boil.
9. Reduce heat and simmer covered until potatoes are cooked, about 20 minutes.
10. Add in corn and peas and simmer until cooked.
11. Taste the soup and season with salt, pepper, garlic powder, cayenne pepper and onion powder until the desired flavor is reached.

Notes

_____
_____
_____
_____
_____
_____
_____
_____
_____
_____
_____
_____

Salad Dressing

Olive Oil
Apple cider vinegar
Coarse sea salt
Fresh cracked black pepper
Italian season blend (see seasoning blends above)
Minced garlic
Lemon juice

1. Place in a bottle and shake!
2. Add more or less of any of the ingredients.

Notes
_____
_____
_____
_____
_____
_____
_____
_____
_____

Courting with Food

It wasn't till I was midway through the preliminary writing of this book that I realized that my now husband and I began our courtship with food. Like most days, I had prepared a small feast for my village and this handsome guy that I was introduced to through a co-worker was going to stop by on his lunch break for a short visit. While on his way to see me, he called to let me know that he was not coming alone as he had a training officer in his patrol car with him. Can you guess what I did? I immediately pulled out the aluminum foil and storage containers to pack him a delicious to-go feast! He sat right there in his patrol car in the parking lot of my apartment complex and enjoyed that meal as I talked his ear off about everything that I could think of.

In that moment it never crossed my mind that this gesture was showing him that I knew how to cook, I interpreted the situation as two officers using their lunchbreak to come and visit me, so the least I could do was provide him a meal.

I still love cooking for him.

xoxo

Hard Boiled Eggs

1. Place eggs in a large pot in a single layer.
2. Fill the pot with cold water until it covers the eggs by 1 inch.
3. Add a pinch of salt.
4. Bring the water to a strong, rolling boil.
5. As soon as it comes to a strong boil, boil for 2-3 minutes (time this so that you don't overcook the eggs)
6. After 2-3 minutes remove pot from heat and cover.
7. Let the eggs sit in the hot water for 10-15 minutes. They will continue cooking. Do not remove the lid.
8. Pour off the water and add cold water. Let the eggs sit in the cold water to cool off.
9. To speed up the cooling process, add ice to the water.
10. Peel the eggs starting at the bottom (widest part).

Notes

_____

_____

_____

_____

_____

_____

_____

Deviled Eggs

12 large eggs
1/2 cup sour cream
1 tsp Dijon mustard
1 tsp Mayo
1/2 tsp salt
Pinch black pepper
1/4 to 1/2 tsp granulated garlic
1/4 to 1/2 tsp. onion powder
3 to 4 strips of bacon (Fry to desired crispiness, chop into small pieces and set aside)
1 1/2 tbsp. chopped green onion.
Ground paprika, to garnish.

1. Peel the eggs.
2. Slice each egg in half.
3. Scoop out the egg yolks and place them in a bowl.
4. Using a fork, smash the yolks into small pieces.
5. Add the sour cream, mayo, mustard, onion powder, pepper, salt and granulated garlic and mix until you get a smooth mixture.
6. Taste the filling and adjust the seasonings to your liking.
7. Fill a sandwich bag with the egg yolk mixture. If you don't have a
8. sandwich or piping bag on hand, you can also just spoon in the egg yolk mixture into the egg white halves.
9. Snip off one of the bottom corners and pipe the egg yolk mixture into the egg white halves.
10. Sprinkle each egg with green onions, paprika, and bacon bits.

Stuffed Bell Peppers

4 bell peppers sliced in half length-wise seeds and membranes removed
1 cup Basmati rice
2 cups broth of your choice
1 tbsp. butter
1 thyme sprig
½ cup white onions diced
1 tbsp. garlic minced
1 lb plain ground sausage (pork or turkey)
1 10 oz can diced tomatoes
2 tsp. parsley
1 cup Colby Jack cheese shredded
1 cup cheddar cheese shredded

1. Bring a pot of salted water to boil.
2. Add peppers and blanch them until they are slightly tender.
3. Remove peppers from water and carefully dry them with a paper towel. Set aside.
4. In a medium-size pot, stir together rice, broth, butter and thyme.
5. Bring to a boil.
6. Immediately reduce heat to a simmer, cover and cook for 15-20 minutes or until water is absorbed. (careful not to overcook)
7. Remove rice from heat, uncover and fluff rice. Set aside.
8. Heat a large, deep skillet greased with olive oil.
9. Add onions and cook until tender.
10. Add garlic and cook until fragrant.
11. Add ground sausage and cook until done.
12. Drain grease.
13. Stir in rice, tomatoes, parsley and Colby jack cheese.
14. Taste and add seasonings if needed (mixture will taste a bit salty but the peppers will balance it out)
15. Stuff peppers generously with filling.
16. Place peppers in a casserole dish.
17. Sprinkle with remaining cheese.
18. Bake at 350 F. for 20- 25 minutes or until cheese is melted and peppers are fork tender.
19. Serve immediately.

Notes
_____
_____
_____
_____

Mac and Cheese

2 cups water
1 1/2 cups chicken broth
5 oz evaporated milk
3/4 cup whole milk divided
3 cups elbow macaroni uncooked
2 tablespoons butter
1 cup sharp cheddar cheese
1 1/2 cups mild white cheddar cheese
1/8 tsp. smoked paprika.
1/4 tsp. ground mustard (TRUST ME)
Salt & Pepper

*When cooking with stainless steel,
immediately wash when done cooking.
This surface cleans better when warm.*

#letseatintentionally

1. In a large deep skillet, add water, chicken broth, evaporated milk, 1/2 cup of whole milk, and elbow macaroni.
2. Bring to a boil and immediately reduce heat to a simmer. (Watch carefully)
3. Cook until al dente while stirring constantly.
4. Remove from heat and let sit for a few minutes until some of the liquid has absorbed.
5. Stir in butter.
6. Add the cheeses a little at a time while stirring.
7. Add in enough of remaining milk to create a creamy sauce. (You can place the pot back on the heat on low if you need more heat to melt the cheese)
8. Stir in smoked paprika and ground mustard.
9. Stir in salt and pepper to taste.
10. Serve immediately.

Notes
_____
_____
_____
_____
_____
_____
_____
_____
_____
_____
_____

Add salt and olive oil to your pasta water as it is coming to a boil.

XOXO

Cajun Garlic Butter Seafood Sauce

Pour over steamed or boiled seafood

Salted butter
Minced Garlic
Olive Oil
Hot Sauce
Lemon Juice
Chicken Broth
Kosher Salt
Seafood Seasoning Blend
Parsley
Add everything to your taste and consistency preference to a pot heat on medium/high til butter is melted and sauce is fragrant.

Notes

_____
_____
_____
_____
_____
_____
_____
_____

Fried Green Tomatoes

2 medium-sized green tomatoes
1 tsp. salt
½ tsp. Cajun seasoning blend (see seasoning blend section p. 16)
1/4 teaspoon black pepper
1 cup all-purpose flour
1 cup buttermilk
1 egg
1 cup seasoned breadcrumbs
1 ¼ cup yellow cornmeal
Vegetable oil for frying

1. Slice tomatoes into 1/4- 1/2-inch slices.
2. Place tomatoes on several layers of paper towels.
3. Mix together salt, Cajun blend (p.16) , and black pepper in a small bowl.
4. Sprinkle tomatoes generously with spice mixture (may not need all of it) and let sit for about 10-15 minutes to allow the extra tomato juices to drain out.
5. Meanwhile, prepare your dredging station. In one bowl, add the flour.
6. In another bowl mix together the buttermilk and egg.
7. In the last bowl, mix together the breadcrumbs and yellow cornmeal.
8. Start by dipping the tomatoes slices into the flour on both sides and shaking off the excess flour. (be sure to get the sides as well)
9. Lay the slices into the egg mixture until both sides are coated with the mixture and flour no longer shows.
10. Place the tomato slices into the breadcrumb mixture and press to coat both sides evenly.
11. Let tomatoes sit for about 5 minutes to allow the coating to set.
12. Heat oil in a skillet until hot. (Do a test with a bread crumb first to make sure the oil is at the right temperature. The breadcrumb should begin to fry evenly immediately when placed in the oil.)
13. Place tomatoes into the skillet, without crowding the pan.
14. Fry each side for about 4-5 minutes until golden brown.
15. Place on a cooling rack with paper towels below to absorb the excess oil that drips off.
16. Serve hot.

Label leftovers with the date or occasion and meal
name before freezing them.
Leftovers taste better when heated in
the oven or the air fryer.

#letseatintentionally

Family Meal Favorites

_____
_____
_____
_____
_____
_____
_____
_____
_____
_____
_____
_____
_____
_____
_____
_____
_____
_____

Family Meal Favorites

_____
_____
_____
_____
_____
_____
_____
_____
_____
_____
_____
_____
_____
_____
_____
_____
_____
_____
_____

Family Meal Favorites

Family Meal Favorites

Family Meal Favorites

Teaching Children to Cook

As a child, no one ever sat me down and taught me how to measure liquids and solids. Which is a key step in cooking and baking. I learned the cooking basics in my junior high school home economics class. It is important that you introduce your children to cooking by letting them prepare their own meals using the appropriate utensils and cooking appliances.

The following recipes are kid-friendly, however adult supervision is required.

Instill in your children that knowing the basics of cooking is an essential life skill.

XOXO

Let's Eat

CHILD-FRIENDLY MEALS

Grilled Hazelnut and Marshmallow Sandwich

4 slices soft white bread
2 tbsp. hazelnut spread
40 mini marshmallows
2 tbsp. butter, divided

1. Spread hazelnut spread on two slices of bread, 1 tablespoon on each slice.
2. Spread marshmallows out evenly on the other two slices, 20 on each slice. Pair them together to make two sandwiches.
3. Melt ½ tbsp. of butter in the skillet or griddle over medium-low heat.
4. Put one sandwich in the skillet and cook until the underside is golden brown.
5. Add another half a tablespoon of butter to the skillet, flip the sandwich and cook until both sides are golden brown and the marshmallows are melted.
6. Wait a minute before slicing, the filling is hot.

Notes
_____
_____
_____
_____

Pigs in a Blanket

1 package (8 count size) hot dogs or smoked sausage links
1 can (8 count size) refrigerated crescent roll dough
4 slices American Cheese, cut in half (optional)

1. Unroll the crescent roll dough and separate it along the perforations to form individual triangles.
2. Place a hot dog on the wide end of each triangle and roll up the dough around it like a crescent roll, pressing the point of the short end to seal the dough.
3. Place the pigs in a blanket on an ungreased baking sheet.
4. Bake at 400 degrees for 10-15 minutes or until the dough is golden brown.
5. Serve warm with ketchup and mustard for dipping.

Notes _____
_____
_____
_____
_____
_____
_____
_____

Pizza Bagels

And you thought bagels were only for breakfast.

1 bag mini bagels
16 oz mozzarella cheese
13 oz jar pizza sauce
Choice of toppings

1. Slice bagels in half
2. Add pizza sauce
3. Add cheese
4. Add desired toppings (Mini pepperoni, turkey sausage crumbles…)
5. Place in air fryer or toaster over till cheese melts

Notes

_____
_____
_____
_____
_____
_____
_____
_____
_____
_____
_____

Do pineapples go on pizza?

Additional Kid-Friendly Meals

- Mini sandwiches prepared on Hawaiian rolls (hot or cold)
- Chicken/Tuna salad
- Fruit salad
- Pasta with marinara
- Sloppy Joes
- Bacon wrapped asparagus

Notes

_____
_____
_____
_____
_____
_____
_____
_____
_____
_____
_____
_____
_____

_____
_____
_____
_____
_____
_____
_____
_____
_____
_____
_____
_____
_____
_____
_____
_____
_____
_____
_____

Snap a pic of your young chef
and place the photo here:

_____
_____
_____
_____
_____
_____
_____
_____
_____
_____
_____
_____
_____
_____
_____
_____
_____
_____

Family Recipes and Notes

_____
_____
_____
_____
_____
_____
_____
_____
_____
_____
_____
_____
_____
_____
_____
_____
_____
_____
_____

Family Recipes and Notes

Go-To Desserts

I have learned through trial and error, that when it comes to desserts most people like what they like and don't usually experiment.

DESSERTS

*Perfect your go-to dessert
and leave the more complicated
sweet treats to experienced bakers.*

XOXO

7-Up Pound Cake

1 cup unsalted butter softened
½ cup butter-flavored shortening
3 cups granulated sugar
5 large eggs room temperature
1 tsp. vanilla extract
1 tsp. lemon extract
3 cups all-purpose flour sifted
½ tsp. salt
¼ cup heavy whipping cream
1 cup 7-Up soda
½ cup all purpose flour (for bundt pan coating)

GLAZE (optional)

1 cup powdered sugar
2 tablespoons 7-up
Mix together until all powdered sugar is dissolved

1. Preheat oven to 325 F.
2. Generously grease and lightly flour a bundt pan. Set aside.
3. In a large bowl, cream together butter, shortening and sugar.
4. Mix in the eggs one at a time.
5. Fold in the vanilla extract and lemon extract.
6. Gradually add in the flour and salt and mix until combined.
7. Mix in the whipping cream and 7-up until well combined and batter is fluffy.
8. Spoon batter into bundt pan.
9. Bake for 1 hour and 10-15 minutes (check after the 1 hour mark) or until knife inserted into middle comes out clean.
10. Let cake sit in pan until pan is warm to the touch.
11. Remove from pan and place on a cooling rack until completely cooled.
12. Drizzle with 7-up glaze if desired.
13. *This cake can also serve as the base for a delicious fruit shortcake. Top with fresh strawberries, a scoop of vanilla ice-cream and a dollop of whipped cream.

Notes

_____

_____

_____

_____

_____

_____

_____

Peach Cobbler

PEACH COBBLER FILLING:

2 (20 oz.) bag of frozen peaches (thawed)
½ cup white sugar
2 tbsp. cornstarch
1 tsp. lemon juice
½ tsp. cinnamon
¼ tsp. nutmeg
Pinch of salt

1. Preheat oven to 375 °F.
2. Combine thawed peaches and filling ingredients in a large skillet over medium heat. Cook until peaches start to soften.
3. Spread peach filling mixture out evenly into the bottom of a baking dish that has been sprayed with non-stick cooking spray or coated with butter flavored shortening.
4. Bake peach filling mixture in preheated oven for 10 minutes while preparing the topping.

Notes
_____
_____
_____

PEACH COBBLER TOPPING:

6 tbsp. unsalted butter room temperature, cut into cubes
1 ½ cups flour
1/2 cup white sugar
1 ½ tsp. baking powder
1 tsp. salt
1/2 cup milk
1 large egg

1. Whisk together flour, sugar, baking powder, and salt in a large bowl.
2. Add cubed butter and use a pastry cutter or fork to combine with the dry ingredients until a coarse crumb form.
3. Pour in milk and mix until just combined and the batter starts to stick together.
4. Grab 2-3 tablespoons of the topping at a time and press together lightly. Place on top of the peach filling mixture. Repeat until all topping is spread across the peaches. It's OK if you have some gaps between the topping.
5. Whisk together 1 egg with 1 tablespoon of milk. Using a pastry brush, brush a light layer of this egg wash onto the topping and sprinkle with additional sugar.
6. Bake cobbler in oven for 30-40 minutes or until topping is golden.
7. Immediately serve with vanilla ice cream.

Skillet Pineapple Upside Down Cake

Do not let your cast iron skillet dry out and rust. After cleaning, always rub it with vegetable oil.

CAKE TOPPING:

1 (20 oz.) can of pineapple rings
4 tbsp. Unsalted butter
3/4 cup packed light brown sugar
1 jar Maraschino cherries

1. Melt butter in 9 inch cast iron skillet
2. Stir in sugar then turn off heat and allow to cool for 10 mins
3. Arrange the pineapple rings and cherries evenly in the skillet, set aside.

CAKE:

1 ½ cup self-rising flour
pinch of salt
2 eggs
1 cup of sugar
1 stick of butter (softened)
¼ cup milk
¼ cup pineapple juice
1 tsp. vanilla extract

1. Preheat the oven to 350 degrees
2. Blend butter and sugar together for 2 mins
3. Separate egg yolks from the whites; reserve the whites
4. Beat in the egg yolks one at a time
5. Add in the vanilla
6. Add flour/salt gradually alternating with the liquids (milk and pineapple juice)
7. Mix whites in a separate bowl until frothy and stiff peaks form
8. Fold the whites into the batter.
9. Pour batter over the topping; spread evenly
10. Bake for 45-50 mins or until a toothpick inserted into the center of the cake comes out clean
11. Glide a butter knife around the edge of the cake to loosen it from the sides of the skillet
12. Allow to cool for 20 mins
13. Flip onto a cake plate

Homemade Whipped Cream

1 cup heavy cream
1 tsp. vanilla extract
1 tbsp. powdered sugar

1. Place mixing bowl in your freezer for 30 to 60 minutes prior to mixing.
2. Using your mixer, in a large bowl, whip cream until stiff peaks are just about to form.
3. Beat in vanilla and sugar until peaks form. Make sure not to over-beat.

Notes
_____
_____
_____
_____
_____
_____
_____
_____
_____
_____

Recipes on the Counter

Think back to your great grand parents and how they always had a little "rolodex style" recipe box on their kitchen counter. Yes, they knew most of the family recipes by heart, but that little box of handwritten notes was always close by should they forget a step.

This handwritten meal journal can now be shared with family and friends. Even passed down to the next generation. This collection of recipes and modifications can also be used to teach your children how to prepare their favorite meals according to your exact steps. This is a small example of how family traditions begin.

As my Scribe Coach Penda says, "InSCRIBE your family legacy" and create a family heirloom.

Family Recipes and Notes

_____

_____

_____

_____

_____

_____

_____

_____

_____

_____

_____

_____

_____

_____

_____

_____

_____

Family Recipes and Notes

_____
_____
_____
_____
_____
_____
_____
_____
_____
_____
_____
_____
_____
_____
_____
_____
_____
_____

Family Recipes and Notes

_____
_____
_____
_____
_____
_____
_____
_____
_____
_____
_____
_____
_____
_____
_____
_____
_____
_____

Family Recipes and Notes

_____
_____
_____
_____
_____
_____
_____
_____
_____
_____
_____
_____
_____
_____
_____
_____
_____
_____
_____

Family Recipes and Notes

_____

_____

_____

_____

_____

_____

_____

_____

_____

_____

_____

_____

_____

_____

_____

_____

_____

Family Recipes and Notes

Family Recipes and Notes

_____
_____
_____
_____
_____
_____
_____
_____
_____
_____
_____
_____
_____
_____
_____
_____
_____

Family Recipes and Notes

Family Recipes and Notes

Family Recipes and Notes

_____
_____
_____
_____
_____
_____
_____
_____
_____
_____
_____
_____
_____
_____
_____
_____
_____
_____

Family Recipes and Notes

_____

_____

_____

_____

_____

_____

_____

_____

_____

_____

_____

_____

_____

_____

_____

_____

_____

_____

Family Recipes and Notes

Family Recipes and Notes

Family Recipes and Notes

Family Recipes and Notes

Family Recipes and Notes

_____
_____
_____
_____
_____
_____
_____
_____
_____
_____
_____
_____
_____
_____
_____
_____
_____

Family Recipes and Notes

_____

_____

_____

_____

_____

_____

_____

_____

_____

_____

_____

_____

_____

_____

_____

_____

_____

Family Recipes and Notes

Family Recipes and Notes

_____

_____

_____

_____

_____

_____

_____

_____

_____

_____

_____

_____

_____

_____

_____

_____

_____

Family Recipes and Notes

_____
_____
_____
_____
_____
_____
_____
_____
_____
_____
_____
_____
_____
_____
_____
_____
_____
_____

Family Recipes and Notes

_____
_____
_____
_____
_____
_____
_____
_____
_____
_____
_____
_____
_____
_____
_____
_____
_____

Family Recipes and Notes

Family Recipes and Notes

_____

_____

_____

_____

_____

_____

_____

_____

_____

_____

_____

_____

_____

_____

_____

_____

_____

Family Recipes and Notes

Family Recipes and Notes

_____

_____

_____

_____

_____

_____

_____

_____

_____

_____

_____

_____

_____

_____

_____

_____

_____

Acknowledgements

I want to take the time out to acknowledge the hardworking women and men who day in and day out show up for their family intentionally. Everyday will not be perfect, every meal will not taste amazing, and everyone will not always agree, but continue to show intentional love and I promise the result will be rewarding. Run your own race, do not become jaded by the past. You can create the life you want to live based upon whatever terms you decide.

Parenting is hard, and marriage is hard. Allow this book to serve as a journal to capture moments in time that you can refer back to when you need to be reminded of your "Why."

Strive toward intentional togetherness, intentional communication, and intentional love.

XOXO

~ShaVonne Cammack

About the Author

ShaVonne Cammack is a North Omaha, Nebraska native, but has been a self-proclaimed "Southern Lady" since 2002 residing in North Alabama. A proud graduate of Alabama A&M University, ShaVonne maintains a rewarding career in the "Rocket City" of Huntsville, AL while loving and caring for her husband and two beautiful children. When she is not cooking, ShaVonne enjoys hiking various trails around Alabama, Georgia, and Tennessee with her social group "Ladies Night Out" and going to football games with her husband.

Connect with us today: www.letseatbook.com
Follow the conversation on Instagram: #letseatintentionally

Made in the USA
Columbia, SC
21 May 2021

38346124R00084